fresh
in winter

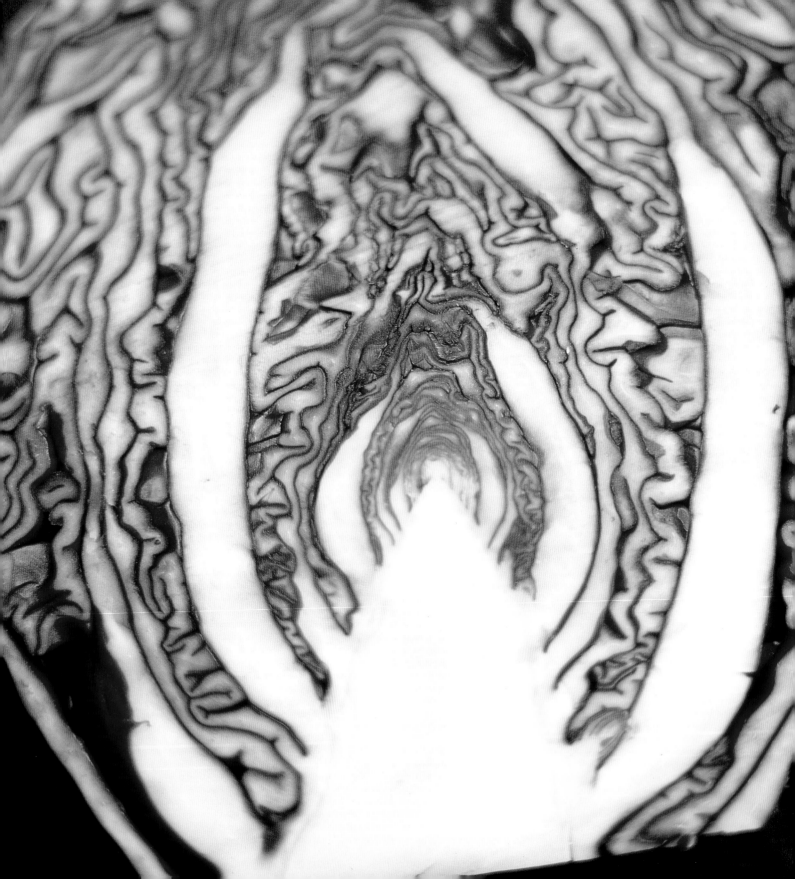

fresh
in winter

cooking with Alastair Hendy
photography by David Loftus

Macmillan Canada

Toronto

First published in Canada in 2000
by Macmillan Canada,
an imprint of CDG Books Canada

Text © Alastair Hendy 1999
Design and photographs
© Ryland Peters & Small 1999

Printed and bound in China by Toppan Printing Co.

Canadian Cataloguing in Publication Data

Hendy, Alastair
  Fresh in winter

Includes index.
ISBN 0-7715-7663-3

1. Cookery. 2. Winter. I. Title.

TX714.H4625 2000   641.5'64   C99-932428-4

Special sales

This book is available at special discounts for bulk
purchases by your group or organization for sales
promotions, premiums, fundraising and seminars. For
details, contact: CDG Books Canada Inc., 99 Yorkville
Avenue, Suite 400, Toronto, ON, M5R 3K5

Notes
Cooking and eating wrongly identified mushrooms can
be fatal. If in doubt, don't. Neither the author nor the
publishers can ever accept any legal responsibility or
liability for any errors, omissions, or mistaken
identification of fungus species that may be made.
All spoon measurements are level unless otherwise noted.
Specialty Asian ingredients are available in large
supermarkets, Thai, Chinese, Japanese, and
Vietnamese shops, as well as Asian stores.
Raw or partly cooked eggs should not be served to the
very young, the old, the frail, or to pregnant women.

1 2 3 4 5 RPS 04 03 02 01 00

To the memory of my grandmother and grandfather
and their vegetable garden at Battle, Sussex.

They taught me so much, without my realizing it at the time.

contents

What's in and what's out? These days, seasonally speaking, this question is a tricky one. A whole year of fruit and vegetables, which once fell into four distinct seasons, now arrives weekly, air freight, from all over the world. Seasons have been blurred. If you forget which harvest comes when, as I do, here are a few pointers to help you spot seasonal produce: it will be piled high because there's lots of it; it will look vibrant because it's absolutely fresh; and it should be about half the usual price because it's probably home-grown—and plentiful. Winter's fresh vegetables come from the earth. This is cabbage, root, and onion season. Whiskery roots and densely fleshed tubers; tight onion bulbs and fat squeaky leeks; heavy crimson cabbages and crisp-hearted greens. Winter's fruits are an exception to the home-grown rule (unless you live in states like Florida or California). Citrus is ripened under the hot sun, sharpened by the first frosts, and keeps well into winter. Tropical fruits also satisfy winter appetites for sweet flavors. Bleak days stir up the love for real home-style cooking. Nothing beats braised cabbage with well-cooked sausages, or a pie filled with melting beef and rich onion gravy, topped with a thick crunchy crust. These are real winter warmers—the stuff of hibernation and nights spent in—but jaded appetites can then be refreshed with clear soups, fish, citrus sauces, and winter salads, antidotes for whenever you've gone overboard on all that homey stuff. This book has the food you want to make in winter. It includes recipes for everyday cooking as well as ideas for elegant entertaining, and endless possibilities for mixing and matching dishes. In each recipe the season's fruits or vegetables remain key—when a leek, beet, lime, or mango tastes wonderful, it should, after cooking, still taste of what it is, only enhanced by what has been added. Take pleasure in the best. Look forward to, anticipate, and relish the food of the season—it will keep your spirits high.

7

Cabbage at last gets good press. This may be because we now know how to use it. Gone are the days of boiling beyond recognition. Much maligned, it was force-fed to us at school under the guise of "greens are good for you." If there had been an ounce of chlorophyll left in it, a vestige of green about it, then perhaps so. No wonder cabbage has taken so long to be lifted from its watery grave. There's nothing wrong in cooking cabbage for a long time, as long as it's the tight, heavy-hearted, red or white sort. It must be slow-braised with just a few tablespoons of liquid (plus fat and other flavorings) so that all the goodness is caught—it loves to be left alone to stew in its own juices.

Cabbages are brassicas—a very large group of related plants that includes cauliflower, broccoli (including calabrese and purple sprouting), and, strangely enough, turnips and kohlrabi. Treated now with the respect they deserve, the sweet hearts of green, red, and white now take center stage. Such is the demand for this regenerated vegetable that an increasing number of varieties now reaches our markets. Cavolo nero (Italian black cabbage) is one—slender shuttlecock-shaped heads of plumelike crinkly dark leaves that need the briefest of cooking. They are excellent in pasta and with anchovies. Savoy cabbages too are now very popular, their deliciously green, crimped leaves are particularly sweet; tossed with butter they'll go with anything, including fish.

Brussels sprouts are like doll-sized cabbages. Although not strictly cabbages, they are of the same family and taste and look like tiny concentrated versions of their larger relatives. Adore them or hate them, there's no in-between—and the Christmas turkey shouldn't be seen without them.

obages

Caesar greens
with anchovy baked toast

Italian cavolo nero (black cabbage), if you can find it, is a fine sweet cabbage that needs only the simplest of cooking. Use another kind if unavailable. However, it is very good with anchovies and with this creamy Parmesan dressing and salty anchovy baked toasts. "Eat up your greens"—happily.

mixed open-heart winter greens, cavolo nero if possible, trimmed and tough stems removed

⅔ cup fresh, finely grated Parmesan cheese,

Anchovy baked toast:

butter, for spreading

1 baguette, thinly sliced diagonally

1 small can anchovy fillets, puréed with a dash of Worcestershire sauce

Creamy dressing:

2 egg yolks

1 garlic clove, crushed

2 tablespoons sherry vinegar

¾ cup olive oil

2 tablespoon light cream

sea salt and freshly ground black pepper

Serves 4

1

For the dressing, beat the egg yolks in a bowl with the garlic, vinegar, and seasoning. Beat in the olive oil thoroughly, then the cream.

2

To make the toasts, butter the baguette slices, arrange on a baking tray, and cook in a preheated oven at 375°F until crisp. Spread thinly with the anchovy mixture.

3

Blanch the greens in boiling salted water for about 1 minute (tougher greens will need 5 minutes). Drain and toss with the dressing and sprinkle heavily with the Parmesan. Serve the greens piled onto the anchovy toasts.

Variations:

• Finely slice the greens and toss into cooked pasta with the dressing, the Parmesan, and finely chopped anchovy fillets.

• Dip veal escalopes in seasoned flour, then in beaten egg, then in breadcrumbs. Sauté in butter on both sides. Add 4 finely chopped canned anchovies to the dressing. Serve the schnitzel with the Caesar greens.

Savoy, ham, and bean terrine

Savoy, the sweetest of the cabbage family, is delicious cold. The ham and beans are best cooked the day before and left to cool in their juices—the meat relaxes and regains its liquid and the beans are stopped from splitting. You can also serve the beans, ham, and cabbage hot instead of as a terrine.

1 fresh bouquet garni of bay leaf, parsley, and thyme

2 onions, halved

3 whole cloves

4 garlic cloves

1 small ham hock (about 2 lb.) or a 1 lb. piece of ham, soaked in water overnight, then drained

1 cup dried haricot beans, soaked in water overnight, then drained

2 sheets leaf gelatin

large leaves from 1 Savoy cabbage

3 canned cooked pimientos, drained and sliced

1 teaspoon green peppercorns

sea salt, to taste

To serve:

¼ cup olive oil

½ tablespoon Dijon, German or wholegrain mustard

balsamic vinegar

a small bunch of chives

Serves 4–8

6-cup loaf pan, plus a smaller pan, for weighting

1

Put the bouquet garni, onions, cloves, garlic, and ham in a saucepan. Cover with cold water, bring to a boil, and skim off any foam. Reduce the heat and simmer very gently for 1½ hours. Add the beans and simmer for 1½ hours until the beans and ham are very tender. Let cool, then remove the ham to a plate.

2

Flake the ham into small chunks. Discard the bouquet garni and onions. Put the gelatin in a dish, cover with water, and leave for 3 minutes or until soft. Strain 1 cup of the bean cooking liquid into a saucepan (discard the remainder but reserve the beans). Reheat with the softened gelatin, then let cool but not set.

3

Blanch the cabbage leaves in boiling salted water for 2 minutes. Drain, pat dry with paper towels, and cut the leaves in half and remove the mid rib.

4

Line the pan with plastic. Add an overlapping layer of leaves, overhanging the pan edge. Add a layer of ham, pimiento, and beans. Season with salt and green peppercorns. Continue layering until full, then add the prepared bean juices until the pan is almost full. Cover with the overhanging leaves and plastic. Top with the second pan and weigh down using full cans or other weights. Chill overnight.

5

Remove the weights, pull back the plastic, and upturn the terrine onto a board or serving dish. Gently pull on the plastic to ease the terrine out of the tin.

6

Beat the oil into the mustard. Slice the terrine and serve at room temperature with the mustard oil, balsamic vinegar, and chives.

Lobster with Louisiana slaw

Lobster with cabbage? You may feel such luxury should not be wasted on cabbage. The luxurious and the humble are often made for each other—just think of caviar and toast or white truffle and potato. And this is delicious; the white cabbage slaw is smoky, creamy, and piquant. Crawfish or mud bugs (crayfish) fished from the bayous are Louisiana's most common crustacea—if you prefer, use them or succulent langoustine or shrimp instead of lobster.

3 red bell peppers or 3 canned cooked pimientos, drained and thinly sliced

2 cooked lobsters or 12 cooked crawfish or large shrimp

1 lemon, quartered, to serve (optional)

Louisiana slaw:

½ white cabbage, cored and finely sliced

1 tablespoon capers, rinsed and drained

1 garlic clove, crushed

2 teaspoons smoked Spanish paprika or regular paprika

¼ teaspoon mustard powder

1 teaspoon Tabasco or to taste

a dash of Worcestershire sauce

1 tablespoon tomato ketchup

3 tablespoons mayonnaise

2 tablespoons freshly squeezed lemon juice

salt and freshly ground black pepper

Serves 4

1

Roast the peppers in a preheated oven at 400°F for about 20 minutes. Remove to a bowl, cover with a plate, and let cool. Rub off the skin, deseed, and remove the inner white ribs. Thinly slice the flesh.

2

Split the cooked lobsters lengthwise. Pull off the legs and remove and discard the head. Crack the lobster claws but leave intact.

3

Mix the slaw ingredients together in a bowl, then add the peppers and stir to mix.

4

Divide the lobsters, crawfish, or shrimp and the slaw between 4 bowls or plates and add a lemon wedge, if using.

Variations:

• Add herbs such as mint, basil, cilantro, or tarragon.

• To serve as a cocktail, add a dash of Cognac, halve the amount of cabbage, and add finely sliced iceberg lettuce.

Vinegared cabbage salad

with seared beef and peanuts

Okay, so I've used a few "out of season" baby tomatoes here—because the dressing is strong and will pump them with flavor and they're good with the beef and cabbage. If you want to be seasonally purist, leave them out. The cabbage can be mixed with the dressing the night before (it will develop a vivid red color). Stir in the tomatoes and bean sprouts just before serving.

8 oz. beef fillet

olive oil, for rubbing

2 tablespoons unsalted blanched peanuts, lightly crushed

1 garlic clove, crushed

2 small hot chiles, seeded and finely chopped

1 tablespoon sugar

2 tablespoons lemon juice

2 tablespoons fish sauce

3 tablespoons rice vinegar

3 cups cored and finely shredded red cabbage

5 small Thai shallots or 1 small red onion, chopped

2 tablespoons grapeseed or peanut oil

16 cherry or baby plum tomatoes

1 cup fresh bean sprouts

3 tablespoons cilantro leaves

Serves 4–6

Variations:

• Add sour cream to the dressing and turn the salad into a slaw. Serve with tuna carpaccio (thinly sliced raw fresh tuna).

• Instead of beef, serve with cooked sliced lamb, chicken, or turkey.

1

Rub the beef fillet with 1 tablespoon of the oil and sear on all sides in a very hot heavy-bottom skillet (about 2 minutes—the fillet should remain uncooked in the middle). Toast the crushed nuts in a dry skillet until lightly browned. Keep turning them as they can easily catch and burn.

2

Put the garlic, chiles, sugar, lemon juice, fish sauce, and vinegar in a bowl and mix until the sugar dissolves. Add the cabbage and shallots or onion and let steep for 1 hour.

3

Mix the vinegared cabbage with the grapeseed or peanut oil, the tomatoes, bean sprouts, cilantro, and 1 tablespoon of the toasted peanuts.

4

Divide between 4–6 bowls. Finely slice the beef and add to the bowls with the remaining peanuts. Pour over any collected dressing in the cabbage salad bowl and serve.

Allspice cabbage

with banana shallots

A chapter on cabbage has to contain braised cabbage. It's the quintessential winter cabbage dish and is so versatile (see variations below). No wonder it's a classic. Red cabbage would be nowhere without it. Banana shallots are so called because of their long shape (nothing like a banana really). This dish can be left for ages in the oven—it will wait for you rather than you for it. (Just put the cooked sausages in the casserole with the cabbage and keep everything on a low heat until you're ready to eat.)

1 red cabbage, halved, cored, and cut into chunks (leaves separated)

4 large banana shallots or 8 shallots, peeled

1 garlic clove, crushed

½ teaspoon crushed cloves

½ teaspoon ground cinnamon

½ teaspoon ground allspice

½ teaspoon freshly grated nutmeg

1½ tablespoons brown sugar

2 tablespoons apple or cranberry jelly

3 tablespoons red wine vinegar

2 tablespoons butter, softened

salt and freshly ground black pepper

8 sausages of your choice, such as regular, herb, game, Italian, or Toulouse

Serves 4

1

Put all the ingredients except the sausages in a heavy casserole dish, add 3 tablespoons water, and mix well.

2

Cover with a lid and braise in a preheated oven at 300°F for 2 hours. Stir twice during the cooking time so the cabbage and shallots receive their fair share of spice and buttery juices.

3

Broil or sauté the sausages until cooked and well browned all over. If the cabbage is not quite ready, put the sausages on top of the cabbage in the casserole to keep hot. If using banana shallots, remove them from the casserole and cut in half lengthwise before serving. Serve with a generous helping of mashed potato with mustard.

Variations:

• Add golden raisins or prunes, chopped chile, and paprika and serve with roast honeyed duck (page 48) or duck confit.

• Add sliced apples and serve with roasted pork or broiled goat cheese.

Christmas turkey for two

with clove stuffing and brussels sprouts

You want turkey on the big day but you don't want the big bird? Easy. You can get the whole Christmas dinner experience with just a drumstick, stuffed then wrapped in bacon. Drumsticks may be considered the poor man's cut, yet the dark meat has all the flavor and the bacon wrapping keeps it moist.

⅔ cup milk

15 whole cloves, lightly crushed

2 bay leaves

1 onion, halved

10 thick slices white bread, crusts removed, processed to crumbs

1 turkey drumstick

6 slices bacon,

1 tablespoon butter

3 cups (about 24) Brussels sprouts (or as many as you wish), outer leaves removed if necessary

salt and freshly ground black pepper

Serves 2

1

Put the milk, cloves, bay leaves, and onion in a small saucepan, bring to a boil, then simmer gently for about 10 minutes. Let cool, then strain into another pan. Finely chop half the cooked onion and add to the milk pan. Discard the rest of the onion, the cloves, and bay leaves.

2

Add the breadcrumbs to the pan, season, and simmer gently, stirring, for about 5 minutes until you have a thick paste.

3

Using a sharp, narrow-bladed knife, bone the turkey drumstick, starting at the thigh end. Release the meat from the bone all the way down inside the leg. Pull out the bone. If you want a piece of bone showing (as shown in the photograph), chop off the end of the bone with a heavy cleaver and reposition it just inside the leg cavity. Stuff the leg with the clove stuffing, secure the opening with toothpicks, and rub with seasoning. Wrap the bacon in overlapping spiraling layers around the leg and put in a roasting pan. Smother with the butter and roast in a preheated oven at 400°F for 50 minutes (cover with foil if the bacon starts to brown too much).

4

Cook the sprouts in boiling salted water for about 6 minutes or until tender (*al dente* is not quite cooked enough for my liking). Drain and toss in some of the turkey pan juices and serve with roasted potatoes and gravy. The leg can be sliced right through into rounds—perfect portion control.

Winter would be miserable without onions. Slow-cooked winter food relies on them so much. All those casseroles, braises, and roasts just couldn't exist without them. Think of such classics as *coq au vin*, bobbing with sweet pickling onions, roasted lamb or chicken tucked with melting cloves of garlic, or a beef pie filled with a caramelized onion gravy—then imagine how harsh winter would be without them. Alliums—onions, garlic, and leeks—are a big family and there are lots of cultivated and wild varieties. Most are grown for their succulent and tightly layered bulbs, pungent hot cloves, or mild stems, while others are picked wild for their garlicky leaves. Our regular globe brown-skinned onion is the all-purpose one and one of the strongest—a real tear-jerker. There are also the milder Spanish, white, and red onions, which can be used raw. Pickling and white pearl onions are best lightly caramelized with a dash of sugar (to accentuate their flavor) and then added to braises or casseroles—or used to make tarts.

Shallots are milder and sweeter than pickling onions and are used for their refined flavor in butter sauces, with seafood, and with expensive cuts of meat. They are the elite of the onion world. Thai shallots are tiny, pink, and very mild—the best in salads. And there's the very long banana shallot which is also pink. Shallots don't keep too well, so enjoy them while they're in season.

Scallions (also known as salad onions or green onions) are an eat-all allium. Grown for their stems and undeveloped bulbs, they're our first-choice salad variety and need the barest of cooking if used in hot dishes.

Non bulb-forming leeks are grown for their pale stems—green parts are usually only used to flavor stock. Earth gets trapped in their stems so wash them well. And there's garlic in all its guises: ordinary white; pink-skinned (one of the best); smoked; elephant garlic (with bulbs as big as your palm, it isn't a garlic at all, but a kind of leek)—and there's fresh garlic and wild garlic leaves too (both appearing in early spring). Always buy bulbs that feel firm and tight. Think of roasted garlic, the rich golden paste squeezed from each papery sleeve onto chargrilled bread and sprinkled with sea salt and olive oil. Now imagine a world without onions. You can't.

onions

Chicken and butter leek soup

This is one of those antidote soups—cleansing, yet nourishing. Perfect for when you have overdone it and are hankering for something light but warm.

6 leeks

1 chicken, about 3 lb., preferably free-range

2 carrots, halved

1 inch fresh ginger, peeled and thickly sliced

2 garlic cloves

2 teaspoons black peppercorns

1 fresh bouquet garni (3 fresh bay leaves tied together with large sprigs of parsley and tarragon)

¼ cup butter

1 tablespoon freshly squeezed lemon juice

a bunch of chives

salt and freshly ground black pepper

Serves 6

1

Slice 2 leeks in half lengthwise and rinse thoroughly under running water to remove all the dirt. Cut the remaining leeks into thick rounds, rinse well, and let soak in a bowl of cold water.

2

Put the chicken in a snug-fitting saucepan, add the halved leeks, carrots, ginger, garlic, peppercorns, and bouquet garni, and season generously. Cover with water, bring to a boil, skim off the foam, turn down the heat, cover, and simmer gently for 45 minutes.

3

Turn off the heat and let the chicken cool completely in the stock.

4

When cold, remove the bird from the pan, flake the meat from the bone, and discard the skin and bones.* Strain the stock and reserve.

5

Put the sliced leeks in a single layer across a wide saucepan. Season, then add the butter and ½ cup of the stock. Heat to simmering, cover, and gently poach for about 5 minutes or until the leeks are tender. Reheat the strained stock with the flaked chicken meat, add the lemon juice, and spoon into bowls. Serve with the poached buttery leeks and a few chive stems.

*__Note:__ If you want to make a richer stock, return the bones to the stock pot, cover, and simmer for 1 hour more, then strain and discard the bones.

Variation:
• Omit the ginger, add broken pieces of pasta to the strained soup stock, and cook as you reheat the chicken (a good way to use up all your dregs of pasta).

25

Cheese and onion flatbread

A bit like a pizza (add anchovies and olives to these flatbreads and you have *pissaladière*), and you can use a pizza base mix to save time. Spanish onions are large but have a gentler onion flavor than ordinary brown ones— they are sweet and need little embellishment. Their fat, even shape makes them ideal for pot-roasting too; they can then be hollowed out and stuffed.

3 garlic cloves, crushed

½ cup butter

4 Spanish onions, quartered and finely sliced lengthwise

⅔ cup curd cheese (preferably goat), grated mild Monterey Jack, or sliced mozzarella

sea salt and freshly ground black pepper

Pizza dough:

1¾ cakes compressed yeast

3⅓ cups all-purpose flour or Italian *tipo 00*

1 teaspoon salt

a large pinch of sugar

fine semolina or extra flour, for dusting

Makes 2 breads

1

To make the pizza dough, dissolve the yeast in 1 cup warm water. Pile the flour on the work surface and make a well in the center. Add the yeast water, salt, and sugar. Mix to make a dough and knead for about 5 minutes until silky and soft. Dust with semolina or flour, put in a bowl, cover, and leave for 1 hour in a warm place until doubled in size.

2

Mash the garlic with the butter. Heat 2 tablespoons of the mixture in a skillet, add the onions, season with salt and pepper, and sauté until just beginning to soften, about 2 minutes. Remove from the skillet.

3

Punch down the risen dough, cut in half, and stretch or roll each half into a loose oval shape. Dust on both sides with semolina or flour, and put back in a warm place to rise for about 15 minutes.

4

Preheat a baking tray in a very hot oven at 450°F.

5

Top the risen breads with a thin layer of cheese, then put the onions on top. Put them on the heated baking tray, brush with the remaining garlic butter, and bake at the same temperature for about 12–15 minutes until puffed and singed.

Variations:

- Instead of cheese, add anchovies and a few sliced black olives.
- Add caraway or fennel seeds to the bread dough.
- In spring, add chopped wild garlic leaves to the curd cheese.

Leek antipasto with mozzarella

You have to be a bit careful when cooking whole leeks; they can be unmanageable and stringy—and trapped dirt can ruin everything. Leeks grow mostly under the surface of the soil (this keeps them pale) and, as they grow, the multi-layered shoots push upward gathering compost between their tightly packed leaves. Choose tender sweet baby leeks for steaming or braising whole. But don't be fooled by their clean outward appearance—slit open the green ends lengthwise and rinse them thoroughly.

12 young leeks, trimmed, and green ends split half-way down, then thoroughly rinsed of all dirt

12 baby mozzarella and/or 4 slices Parma ham

Salsa verde:

a small bunch of flat-leaf parsley

4 sprigs of basil

1 garlic clove, crushed

½ tablespoon capers, rinsed

3 baby gherkins

½ tablespoon white wine vinegar

1 tablespoon freshly squeezed lemon juice

⅔ cup virgin olive oil

4 canned anchovy fillets, drained and finely chopped

Serves 4 as a first course

1

To make the salsa verde, put all the ingredients in a blender or food processor and blend to a coarse purée.

2

Steam the cleaned leeks for about 5 minutes or until tender. Dress with the salsa verde and let cool. Serve with the mozzarella and/or Parma ham.

Variations:

• Wrap mozzarella in prosciutto, roast briefly in a hot oven until the prosciutto begins to caramelize and the cheese starts to melts, then serve with the leeks and salsa verde.

• Serve the leeks with poached eggs and ham or with butter mashed with wholegrain mustard and chopped flat-leaf parsley.

29

Pub beef and onion pies

The best beef and onion pies are found in British pubs. I like this easy hot water crust pastry, but you can use bought shortcrust or puff pastry instead.

¼ cup butter, for frying

2 lb. braising steak, cubed

5 onions, 1 sliced lengthwise, 4 halved and finely sliced

2 dried bay leaves, ground or very finely crumbled

2 tablespoons all-purpose flour

2 teaspoons Worcestershire sauce

2 teaspoons tomato purée

1 teaspoon anchovy sauce

1 tablespoon mushroom sauce

2 cups Guinness Stout

2 teaspoons sugar

1 tablespoon wine vinegar

salt and freshly cracked black pepper

hot English mustard, to serve (optional)

Hot water crust pastry:

3 cups all-purpose flour

a large pinch of salt

¾ cup lard

⅔ cup milk

1 egg yolk, to glaze

Serves 6

6 small rectangular pie dishes

1

Heat 1 tablespoon of the butter in a deep skillet. Season the meat and brown in batches. Remove and keep warm.

2

Heat the remaining butter in the skillet, add the finely sliced onions and bay leaves, and sauté until lightly browned. Season, stir in the flour, adding extra butter if necessary, and sauté until the onion roux is a rich brown.

3

Stir in the Worcestershire sauce, tomato purée, anchovy sauce, mushroom sauce, Guinness Stout, sugar, and vinegar and let bubble for 5 minutes. Stir in 1¼ cups water, cover, and simmer gently for 1½ hours. Spoon into the pie dishes.

4

To make the pastry, sift the flour and salt into a bowl. Put the lard, milk, and ⅔ cup water in a saucepan and bring to a boil. Stir into the flour, let cool, then knead gently but firmly. Use immediately—do not refrigerate.

5

Roll out the pastry to ⅛ inch thick. Cut 6 rectangles to fit the tops of the pie dishes and press an onion slice into each. Cut small strips from the remaining pastry and use to line the rim of each dish, pressing firmly. Place a pastry lid on top and, using your fingers or tip of a knife, press the edges onto the pastry-lined rim to seal. Make a small hole in the top of each pie to let the steam escape, brush with egg yolk, and bake in a preheated oven at 400°F for 30 minutes.

6

Serve with mustard, if using, and boiled potatoes or mashed potatoes.

Pot-roasted red onions

with feta cheese and oregano

Peeled red onions are slow-baked with oregano and olive oil, then served with crumbled feta cheese. I'm not a big fan of quartered roasted onions—they over-caramelize and taste too burnt at the edges. Baking or roasting them whole keeps them succulent and makes the bulbs meltingly tender, full of onion concentrate. You can swap oregano for rosemary, and you can take it even further if you like—see the variations below.

8 small or 6 medium red onions

2 teaspoons dried oregano

4 tablespoons olive oil

12 black olives

leaves from 4 sprigs of oregano

1 cup feta or blue cheese, crumbled

sea salt and freshly ground black pepper

Serves 4

1

Stand the peeled onions in a snug-fitting casserole (with lid) or a roasting pan (use foil as a cover). Sprinkle with dried oregano, spoon over half of the oil, and season generously. Cover and roast in a preheated oven at 350°F for 45–60 minutes or until tender.

2

Remove the lid, put in the olives and a few of the fresh oregano leaves, baste with the remaining olive oil, and return to the oven for 5 minutes. Serve with crumbled feta or blue cheese and the remaining oregano leaves.

Variations:

• Slice the roasted onions into quarters before serving and toss with all the ingredients, plus winter salad leaves, walnuts, a dash of walnut oil, and balsamic vinegar.

• Cut in half lengthwise and put, cut side up, in a gratin dish. Baste with garlic-infused olive oil and herbs, then lightly caramelize under a hot broiler. Serve with mashed sweet potato and broiled lamb cutlets or pork chops.

Rosemary and olive lamb

with roasted garlic lima beans

I've used rack of lamb, but you may prefer leg or shoulder as in the variation. If you've just decided you want to cook this dish today, use canned lima beans instead (omit step 1)—cannellini beans are equally good.

3 cups dried lima beans, soaked overnight in cold water to cover, then drained

1 onion

2 whole heads of garlic, separated into cloves (skin on)

½ bouillon cube (chicken or lamb), crumbled

1 fresh bouquet garni (fresh bay leaves, sprigs of thyme, parsley, and rosemary)

1 rack of lamb (total 12 ribs), trimmed of excess fat

leaves from 1 small bunch of rosemary, chopped

8 black olives, pitted and chopped

2 tablespoons olive oil

sea salt and freshly ground black pepper

Serves 4

1

Put the beans, onion, 4 peeled garlic cloves, bouillon cube, and bouquet garni in a saucepan, cover with cold water, and bring to a boil. Skim off any foam, lower the heat after 5 minutes, and gently simmer for 1 hour or until the beans are tender (season only during the last 10 minutes of cooking). Let cool in the juices. Discard the onion, garlic, and bouquet garni.

2

Rub the lamb with salt and pepper and coat the fat side with the chopped rosemary and chopped olives, pressing on well. Put the rack of lamb in a roasting pan, tuck the unpeeled garlic cloves underneath, and spoon the oil over the top. Roast in a preheated oven at 400°F for 20–25 minutes until the meat is medium-rare, or until cooked to your liking.

3

Meanwhile reheat the beans in their cooking liquid. When the lamb is cooked, remove from the pan, cover with foil, and let rest for 5 minutes. Pop the garlic cloves out of their papery skins, strain the beans, and mix with the roasted garlic cloves in the pan. Transfer to a warmed serving dish. Slice the lamb and place on top of the roasted garlic lima beans.

Variations:

• If using a leg of lamb, roast for 20–25 minutes per pound, adding the garlic to the roasting pan 25 minutes before the end of the cooking time. Let the meat rest for 10 minutes before carving. If you need to keep everything warm, the cooked beans and skinned garlic cloves can be spooned around the lamb in the roasting pan.

• If using shoulder of lamb, open-roast until brown, then put in a casserole and braise with the beans until meltingly tender.

Root vegetables are the fruit of the earth. But they're rarely allowed to take center stage on the plate as other vegetables do. I think we should take a fresh look at our roots. Fattened with sweet goodness and crisped by frost, their smooth flesh is melting and delicate when cooked—and so versatile, too. Potatoes are the favorite and they're one of the world's most important crops. Remember to use "waxy" fleshed ones for boiling, fries, and gratins; and "floury" baking ones for mashing and jacket baking. The potato is nature's perfect package—perfectly nutritious, perfectly delicious, and so easy to cook. Jerusalem artichokes, like potatoes, are tubers. Once very knobbly and difficult to peel, they are now having all their knobbles bred out of them. This has made peeling easy but these "designer" ones don't have the same earthy smoky flavors of the original. Knobbly originals are still out there, thankfully. On to real roots. There are all the long and squat, rooty looking ones: carrots, parsnips, beets, salsify, horseradish (used grated only), and a newcomer, Hamburg parsley root, that tastes like

root

a fabulously herby parsnip. Beets are delicious roots too, even their young leaves can be used in salads. Select smooth-skinned roots that are firm—wrinkles and too much "give" indicate they were probably dug from the earth weeks ago. Then there's the boulder bunch—rutabaga, turnips, and celery root. Celery root has a warty creased exterior but it has inner beauty. Cut away its earthen skin to reveal white firm flesh tasting of mild celery with a fennel twang. Turnips are best young—they become all fibrous if left to mature—and great with duck, especially good in a roast duck tagine or flavored broth along with parsnips and other roots. Rutabagas are fine on the large size, they stay surprisingly tender—excellent as "mashed neeps" the Scottish dish of mashed rutabaga and potato, (celery root is good this way too). All these rooty things are a characterful and delicious bunch.

vegetables

Oven-baked sweet potatoes
with saffron butter and crisp onions

Sweet potatoes—perfect for baking. They caramelize beautifully between skin and flesh, and take less time to bake than regular potatoes. There are two main categories—orange-fleshed and white-fleshed—and there are a number of sub-species within each category. The orange kind is the sweetest.

4 medium orange-fleshed sweet potatoes

½ teaspoon saffron strands

½ tablespoon hot milk

1 cup butter, at room temperature

2 onions, finely sliced

a large pinch of ground cinnamon

½ teaspoon paprika

3 tablespoons olive oil

sea salt and freshly ground black pepper

Serves 4

1

Put the sweet potatoes in a roasting pan and bake in a preheated oven at 400°F for about 40 minutes or until soft to the touch.

2

Sprinkle the saffron onto the hot milk and leave to infuse for about 10 minutes. Mash the saffron milk into the butter.

3

Toss the onions with the spices, salt, and pepper. Heat the olive oil in a skillet, add the onions, and sauté gently until crisp and golden—watch they don't burn at the edges of the skillet. Drain on crumpled paper towels.

4

To serve, split open each potato, then top with saffron butter and crispy onions.

Variations:

• Use any baking potatoes—little ones can be topped with toasted pine nuts and served as an appetizer.

• Use saffron oil instead of butter, then top the sweet potato with creamy sharp curd cheese and torn mint leaves.

Beets: roots and tops
with eggs and horseradish cream dressing

Never peel a beet before you boil him. He'll be a dead beet. You'll lose all the deep red juice to the cooking water—beautiful water, but a sad brown beet. Just rinse off any dirt, cut off the leaves (but leave a small tuft; again, over-trimming will cause him to bleed), and simmer in salted water until tender. Let cool, then rub off the skin—it will slither off (sensuously). Beet leaves are seriously good salad leaves. If they look a bit sad, plunge them into ice water and leave them to soak—this will cheer them up.

16 baby beets or 6 medium, with the fresh leafy tops still attached

12 quail eggs or 4 small hen eggs

1 teaspoon honey

½ tablespoon cider vinegar or lemon juice

2 tablespoons crème fraîche or sour cream

1 inch fresh horseradish root, peeled and finely grated

chives, finely chopped (optional)

sea salt and freshly ground black pepper

Serves 4 as an appetizer

1
Cut off the beet leaves and rinse well. Clean the roots carefully without breaking the skin. Simmer the roots in salted water until tender (20 minutes for small beets or about 1 hour for large ones).

2
Simmer the quail eggs (1 minute for soft yolk, 2 minutes for hard), then plunge into cold water to cool, then peel. If using hen eggs, simmer for about 4 minutes for soft yolk or 6 minutes for hard; peel and cut in half (or quarters if hard-cooked).

3
Dissolve the honey in the vinegar or lemon juice, beat in the crème fraîche and seasoning. Mix in ½ tablespoon grated horseradish. Arrange the leaves, roots, and eggs in shallow bowls, dress with the horseradish cream, and sprinkle with more grated horseradish, chives, if using, salt, and pepper.

Variation:
• Omit the boiled eggs and make a warm beet and potato Caesar salad using the freshly cooked roots, boiled waxy baby potatoes, and the beet leaves. Add Creamy Dressing (page 10), ⅔ cup freshly grated Parmesan and 2 chopped anchovies.

41

Jerusalem artichoke chowder
with bacon and seared scallops

Chowder (a thick white seafood soup flavored with bacon) is traditionally thickened with potato. Using Jerusalem artichokes gives it wintry earthiness, and the scallops elevate the humble soup to restaurant status. Jerusalem artichokes are not artichokes, but tubers like potatoes. Though they look knobbly and earthy, they have a pronounced sweet flavor.

8 large scallops

2 tablespoons olive oil

1 lb. Jerusalem artichokes

2 tablespoons butter

1 leek, white part only, rinsed and finely chopped

1 bay leaf

2 sprigs of thyme

3 potatoes, diced

3 slices bacon

1 cup crème fraîche or sour cream

1¼ cups milk

1¾ cups chicken stock

a squeeze of fresh lemon juice

salt and freshly ground black pepper

Serves 8 as an appetizer, 4 for supper

1
Trim the scallops if necessary and slice in half to make 16 rounds. Season, toss in the olive oil, and set aside.

2
Peel and dice the Jerusalem artichokes and, as you do so, put them into a bowl of water acidulated with a dash of lemon juice to prevent discoloration.

3
Heat the butter in a large saucepan, add leek, bay leaf, and thyme, and sauté until soft. Add the Jerusalem artichokes and potatoes and cook for 1 minute more. Add the bacon, crème fraîche, milk, stock, lemon juice, and seasoning. Bring to a boil, reduce the heat, and simmer for 20 minutes or until soft.

4
Discard the bay leaf and bacon and, using a processor or hand blender (which will give you a "cappuccino" froth), blend to a smooth purée. Add extra stock or milk if it needs thinning, then taste and adjust the seasoning.

5
Heat a heavy-bottom skillet until smoking hot and sear the scallops for 30 seconds on each side. Divide the soup between 4–6 bowls and add slices of seared scallop to each one.

Variation:
• Use freshly steamed cockles instead of scallops. Add them and their juices to the soup.

Thyme buttered baby roots

with homemade horseradish cream

This dish of perfectly cooked tender little roots—tails, tops, and all—is good enough as a course on its own. You can also use grown-up roots, cut to size. Hamburg parsley tastes and looks like baby parsnip, but has a more earthy herby flavor. Salsify is a long narrow hairy root, not the most endearing of objects, but with delicious creamy flesh.

¼ cup butter

4 thyme sprigs

sea salt and freshly ground black pepper

A selection of baby roots, such as:

baby waxy potatoes, unpeeled but scrubbed

baby carrots, unpeeled, trimmed, and scrubbed

baby turnips, scrubbed or peeled if larger

Hamburg parsley root, peeled

salsify or scorzonera, peeled*

rutabaga, peeled and cut into chunks

small parsnips, peeled

Jerusalem artichokes, peeled and cut into chunks*

Homemade horseradish and garlic cream (optional):

⅓ cup crème fraîche or sour cream

1 tablespoon freshly grated horseradish root

2 shallots, finely chopped

2 garlic cloves, crushed

2 tablespoons white wine vinegar

salt and freshly ground black pepper

Serves 4–6

***Note:** Peeled salsify and Jerusalem artichokes should be put into a bowl of acidulated water (water with a dash of lemon juice) to prevent browning. Dip in the lemon water as you peel; it will stop your hands from staining too.*

1

Put all the horseradish cream ingredients in a bowl and beat well. Taste and add a dash more vinegar or seasoning if necessary.

2

Melt the butter and strip the thyme leaves from their stems into the butter and leave to infuse while you cook the roots.

3

Simmer the prepared roots in salted water until cooked (pierce a large one with a knife to test). If certain roots are larger or thicker than others (such as parsnips), start off with them first, and cook for about 8 minutes, then add the smaller, narrower ones (such as baby carrots) and let simmer for a further 3 minutes. Drain and toss with the thyme butter, sea salt, and black pepper. Serve with a spoon of horseradish cream, if using.

Variations:

• Serve thyme buttered roots with:

• Salt beef (poached until tender with carrots, onion, bay leaf, and peppercorns) and freshly grated horseradish.

• Beet aioli (mayonnaise mixed with crushed garlic and cooked puréed beets).

• Pot-Roasted Lemon Poussin (page 58)

• Roast rib of beef (include the horseradish and garlic cream) or with other roasted meats.

Pastrami salmon with caraway celery root

The salmon is flavored with pastrami-cure style ingredients; it semi-cures overnight. If you want to inject loads of flavor, leave the spices and herbs on for a further day or two, but even just 2–4 hours works wonders. Salmon also loves salt (it brings out the flavor and firms up the flesh) and when seared until blackened on both sides, the flavors are intensified. Freshly grated celery roots can be bought in packs from specialty shops.

1½ lb. salmon fillet (middle cut of a large salmon), skin on, pin bones removed

1 tablespoon olive oil

Pastrami cure:

1 tablespoon salt

1 tablespoon sugar

1 teaspoon ground allspice

1 teaspoon paprika

1 teaspoon garlic powder

1 teaspoon onion powder

1 tablespoon wholegrain or mild mustard

2 tablespoons finely chopped chives

2 tablespoons finely chopped dill, plus a few sprigs, to serve

Caraway celery root:

1 celery root (celeriac), about 1 lb.

juice of 1 lemon

2 tablespoons butter

1 shallot, finely chopped

1 teaspoon caraway seeds

½ cup white wine

⅔ cup heavy cream

1 teaspoon mustard powder

salt and freshly ground black pepper

Serves 4

1

To make the pastrami cure, mix all the ingredients in a bowl. Rub it over the flesh side of the salmon, wrap tightly in plastic, put in a shallow dish, weigh down with a food can, and chill overnight.

2

To prepare the celery root, peel it, cut in quarters, and dip in a bowl of water with half the lemon juice to prevent browning. Using a food processor or mandoline, cut into long, fine julienne strips (a normal grater will give you a mush), and immerse in the acidulated water.

3

Drain the celery root. Heat the butter in a small skillet, add the shallot, and sauté until soft and translucent. Add salt, pepper, and caraway seeds and cook for 1 minute without browning. Add the wine and remaining lemon juice and reduce until syrupy. Stir in the cream, mustard powder, and celery root and gently cook until just softened, about 3 minutes. Taste and adjust the seasoning.

4

Scrape the pastrami cure off the salmon and rub with the oil. Heat a heavy-bottom skillet until smoking hot (turn on the extraction fan) and sear the fillet, skin side down, for about 3 minutes. Don't move it—it's meant to blacken, but won't taste burnt. Slide a spatula under the fish, turn it over, and sear for 2 minutes. It should be opaque and undercooked in the middle. Slice into 4 and serve with the caraway celery root.

Root and honey duck hot pot

For this dish, I make my own duck stock out of the pre-roasted duck carcass but you can use four duck pieces and store-bought chicken stock instead. Add potatoes and squash if you want a more substantial meal, or just serve with crusty bread. Double-roasting the duck releases more fat and tenderizes the flesh, a bit like duck confit—roast it just once if you prefer it pink.

1 duck or 4 duck portions

½ teaspoon ground mace or
½ teaspoon freshly grated nutmeg

1 tablespoon honey

2 tablespoons olive oil

1 leek, white and pale green part only, chopped

2 celery stalks (with leaves) or Chinese celery, stalks chopped, leaves reserved

2 garlic cloves, finely chopped

1 teaspoon coriander seeds

½ teaspoons cumin seeds, toasted in a hot dry skillet

4–6 cups well-seasoned chicken stock

1 lb. mixed root vegetables, such as parsnips or Hamburg parsley root, small turnips and salsify, all peeled and with any large roots thickly sliced

a good squeeze of lemon juice

sea salt and freshly ground black pepper

Serves 4

1

If using a whole duck, prick it all over with a sharp knife (plus a few extra stabs around the flanks and fatty parts), rub with salt, pepper, and mace or nutmeg. Place on a rack over a roasting pan, then rub with half of the honey. Roast in a preheated oven at 375°F for 1 hour.

2

Loosely cover with foil, let cool, then cut into quarters. Discard the ribs and backbone or use to make a stock. At this point the duck can be refrigerated for up to 3 days if you wish: it will become wrinkled and pallid, but when re-roasted will turn mahogany brown, plump, and crisp.

3

If using duck portions, slash the skin and fat with a sharp knife and prepare as above. Put in a roasting pan and cook in a preheated oven at 375°F for 40 minutes. Let cool as above.

4

Heat the olive oil in a large skillet, add the chopped leek, celery stalks, garlic, coriander and cumin seeds, and gently sauté until the vegetables have softened but not browned. Add the stock and bring to a boil, stir in the remaining honey, then add the roots and gently simmer for about 25 minutes. Add the lemon juice, then taste and adjust the seasoning.

5

Meanwhile, re-roast the duck portions for 15 minutes at 425°F until crisp and brown. Chop or flake the meat and divide between 4 Chinese-style bowls. Add the soup and vegetables and top with the celery leaves.

Cardamom carrot teacakes

French fancies—little cubes of sweet spongecake garnished with a blob of "cream" and cloaked in candy yellow, bedroom pink, or chocolate fondant—are the cakes of seaside guest houses. And were the cakes, along with similarly colored Battenberg cake, I associate with childhood visits to my grandparents. Packaged cakes still retain a visual magic but now taste just that bit too sweet. So I've created a new model, a minimal French fancy if such a contradiction is possible—a carrot cake flavored with cardamom and coconut, cubed and coated in white frosting. Make sure you make a good strong cup of tea (that's tea with tea leaves, not bags) to go with them.

black seeds from 20 green cardamom pods, lightly bruised

3 cups all-purpose flour

3 cups sugar

1 teaspoon salt

2 teaspoons baking powder

1 teaspoon bicarbonate of soda

2 teaspoons ground cinnamon

1¾ cups peanut oil

4 large eggs, lightly beaten

1 teaspoon vanilla extract

1½ cups walnut pieces, chopped

1½ cups unsweetened shredded coconut

1⅓ cups puréed cooked carrot

Coconut frosting:

⅔ cup canned coconut cream

3 cups confectioners' sugar, sifted

Makes 18

one 6 x 12 inch cake pan

1

Grease and line the base and sides of a 6 x 12 inch cake pan with baking parchment.

2

Sift the dry ingredients into a bowl, make a well in the center, pour in the oil, eggs, and vanilla extract and beat slowly together. Fold in the remaining ingredients and pour into the pan. Bake in a preheated oven at 350°F for 30 minutes. Remove from the oven, invert onto a wire rack, and let cool.

3

Slice the top off the cake and discard, then cut the cake into 18 cubes. Stand the cubes on a wire rack set over a tray. To make the frosting, mix the coconut cream with the confectioners' sugar to make a spreadable paste and spoon over the cubes of cake and smooth to coat. Let set until firm.

Variations:

• To make a cream cheese frosting, beat 1 cup cream cheese until smooth, then beat in 2½ cups confectioners' sugar. Spread over the teacakes.

• Add chopped stem ginger in syrup or poppy seeds to the cake mix.

One exception I make to the home-grown rule is for winter fruits, such as citrus. They bring a much needed taste of the sun to winter and some of them we could not be without. Lemons, for example, personify freshness and enliven everything they touch. Sharp lemon juice and the rounder flavor of the zest can bring sparkling life to vegetables, fish, and meat—and its chemical and acidic properties are indispensable in much of our cooking. Then there are limes. Like lemons but more aromatic and with extra tang. Fabulous in all things Asian. There are some special oranges that are just too good to neglect: the brightly colored Valencia, the seedless navel, the ruby-inked blood orange with raspberry-sweet juice, and the tart, puffy-skinned Seville (for cooking).

Clementines, satsumas, tangerines, mandarins, and ortaniques (an orange and tangerine hybrid) are rarely used in cooking. However, their sweet juice and whole segments are good in desserts and make wonderful homemade

gelatin. Quail-egg-sized kumquats can't be peeled, but are eaten skin and all. They're very sharp so need poaching in syrup first and are very good in relishes to serve with meat and game birds. The huge pomelo, *Citrus grandis*, certainly lives up to its king-sized name. Waxy-smooth and voluptuous, with beautiful lime-ocher skin, it is easy to peel and tastes a little like a crisp, sweet grapefruit. Yellow and pink grapefruit aren't just for breakfast. Tart yet sweet, they're good in salads and make excellent sorbets, too. Citrus fruits are winter's cleansers and purifiers; use them while they're in season, when they're at their best.

s fruits

Smoked fishcakes

with lemon butter spinach

Smoked fish make the best fishcakes. Other fish such as salmon often seem tasteless when mixed with mashed potato and sautéed. I've made champ, the Irish dish of mashed potato infused with scallion, as the base for my cakes. The lemon butter is much easier to make than hollandaise.

1¼ cups milk

1 lb. smoked haddock

¼ cup butter

4 scallions, finely chopped

3 tablespoons heavy cream

1¾ lb. potatoes, cooked in boiling salted water

2 tablespoons chopped parsley

2 tablespoons chopped basil

freshly grated nutmeg

all-purpose flour, for dusting

1 egg, lightly beaten

¼ cup breadcrumbs (from day-old white bread)

vegetable oil, for frying

sea salt and freshly ground black pepper

Lemon butter spinach:

juice of 1 lemon

6 tablespoons butter, chilled and diced

baby spinach, to serve

Makes 12 balls or 6 cakes

1

Heat the milk in a wide shallow saucepan, add the haddock, and poach for about 5 minutes. Remove from the milk and let cool. Flake the fish, removing any bones and skin. Discard the milk.

2

Heat the butter in a small saucepan over a gentle heat, add the scallions and cream, and sauté gently for about 1 minute to soften the scallions. Add the mixture to the cooked potato and mash them together. Mash in the parsley, basil, nutmeg, salt, and pepper. Mix in the flaked fish, then taste and adjust the seasoning and chill in the refrigerator for 1 hour or overnight to firm the mixture.

3

Mold the fish and potato mixture into 12 small balls or 6 large cakes. Flour each cake, dip into the beaten egg, and then pat with breadcrumbs. Chill until needed.

4

Heat the vegetable oil in a deep-fat fryer to the recommended level and temperature. Add the balls in batches and fry for about 3 minutes. Alternatively, heat about ½-inch depth of oil and 1 tablespoon of butter in a large, preferably nonstick, skillet. Add the fishcakes and sauté all over until golden brown. Set aside to keep them warm.

5

Heat the lemon juice in a small saucepan and beat in the chilled butter over a low heat to form an emulsion. Toss with the spinach leaves and serve with the fishcakes.

Kumquat duck with chile citrus sauce

Kumquats or cumquats are sharply tangy and look like cocktail oranges (if there could be such a thing). It's the skin that has the flavor, don't even think of trying to peel one (you'll end up with nothing)—they're the snowpea of the citrus world and are best cooked. If you roast a whole duck (to serve 4), the leg meat can be shredded and used to make spring rolls and any remaining citrus sauce can be used as a dipping sauce.

3 large duck breasts

½ tablespoon honey

¼ cup soy sauce

salt

Chile citrus sauce:

12 kumquats, quartered

1 inch fresh ginger, peeled and grated

3 shallots, finely sliced lengthwise

2 garlic cloves, chopped

3 tablespoons sugar

1 tablespoon fish sauce

2 tablespoons rice vinegar

juice of 4 oranges, preferably blood oranges

juice of 3 limes

juice of 2 grapefruit

2 small red chiles, quartered and seeded

1 tablespoon cornstarch, blended with 2 tablespoons water

To serve:

2 long red mild chiles, seeded and sliced into fine long shreds

watercress (optional)

scallions (optional)

Serves 6

1

Using a sharp knife finely score the duck skin. Mix the honey with the soy sauce. Rub the breasts with a little salt, then with the soy mixture, cover, and chill for at least 30 minutes or overnight.

2

To make the sauce, put the kumquats, ginger, shallots, garlic, sugar, and 1 cup water in a saucepan and fast simmer for about 10 minutes until reduced by half. Stir in the other ingredients, except the cornstarch paste, simmer gently for 5 minutes, then strain the syrup into a clean pan. Return the kumquat peel to the syrup (discard the remaining contents of the strainer). Add the blended cornstarch and boil the syrup for 1 minute to thicken,

3

Roast the duck breasts in a preheated oven at 425°F for 15 minutes or until golden. Let rest for 5 minutes, then slice thickly. Reheat the sauce. Slice the duck, pile into bowls, coat with the sauce, add the sliced chiles and watercress and scallions, if using, and serve with plain boiled rice.

Variations:

• Serve the sauce with crispy reef fish. Score the fish on both flanks with parallel cuts and rub with seasoning. Heat vegetable oil in a deep saucepan and slide in the fish—head first. Fry for 5–8 minutes, then serve dressed with the sauce and sliced shallots.

• Use the duck to make spring rolls, adding cucumber, scallions, sesame oil, soy sauce, and bean sprouts. Roll up in spring roll wrappers and fry in corn oil. Serve with the sauce.

Clay pot lemon poussin

Lemon chicken with buttery garlic rice is my idea of perfect chicken—and putting everything in one pot is perfection too: no juices are lost and you can scrape the cooking dish clean at the table, down to every last caramelized buttery morsel. Using individual pots also makes serving easy as there's no "dishing up"—everything is already portioned. If you haven't got four small pots, you can cook all the birds and the rice in one large pot, then serve on warmed plates.

⅔ cup butter, softened

6 garlic cloves, 4 smashed and 2 crushed

a bunch of parsley, finely chopped

4 unwaxed lemons, juice of 1 and the rest cut into wedges

4 poussin (baby chickens or coquelets), preferably free-range

2 tablespoons olive oil

4 cups rice

sea salt and freshly ground black pepper

Serves 4

1

Mix ½ cup of the butter with the 2 crushed garlic cloves and chopped parsley. Season well.

2

Put 1 wedge of lemon, 1 smashed garlic clove, and 1 heaped teaspoon of the butter mixture inside each chicken and tie the legs together with string. Rub with salt and pepper.

3

Heat the remaining butter with the oil in a large skillet and brown the birds on all sides. Put the birds in the pots.

4

Mix the remaining garlic parsley butter with the rice and distribute around each chicken. Drizzle lemon juice over each bird and tuck in the remaining lemon wedges. Add 1¾ cups water to each pot, cover, and cook in a preheated oven at 425°F for 45—50 minutes. If you want greenery, serve a bowl of green beans for everyone to help themselves.

Variations:

• To make Moroccan lemon chicken, instead of parsley, mix saffron with the butter, add golden raisins and toasted pine nuts to the rice, and bake with preserved lemons instead of fresh. You could also rub the chicken before sautéing with a little paprika, ground cumin, cinnamon, and ginger.

Clementine and orange jewels

A sexy dessert, these gelatin "jewels" are made with pure fresh citrus juice. Slightly tart and very refreshing, I like to make my own, rather than using the store-bought (which tastes too sweet and artificial). If you fancy yours sweeter, taste the juice when the sugar has dissolved and add more sugar to suit. You could always add a few peeled segments of fruit, but I prefer the minimalist look of pure gelatin.

Clementine jewels:

2 cups clementine or tangerine juice (about 14 fruit)

4 heaping tablespoons sugar

4 sheets leaf gelatin

Blood orange jewels:

2 cups blood orange juice (about 8 fruit)

3 tablespoons sugar

4 sheets leaf gelatin

heavy cream, to serve

Serves 4

1

To make the clementine gelatin jewel, strain the juice through a cheesecloth-lined sieve.

2

Put the leaf gelatin in a shallow dish and just cover with water. Soak for a few minutes until softened.

3

Warm the strained juice with the sugar (don't heat too much or you will lose flavor and color). Lift the leaf gelatin from its soaking water and add to the juice. Stir until fully dissolved. Pour into a serving bowl or individual dishes or glasses.

4

Make the blood orange version in the same way, then chill both desserts until set.

Variations:

- Use other citrus juice or mix with champagne for a champagne gelatin.
- Add a few cranberries poached in orange juice, sugar, and Cointreau.

Vodka ice with ginger and blood oranges

Blood oranges, like Sevilles, are strictly seasonal. Unlike Sevilles, their deep red juice is deliciously sweet, and makes one of the best freshly squeezed drinks—or, as here, a granita. This one is easy to put together and will keep people who are programmed to enjoy drink more than food very happy indeed—it's stacked with vodka. Just remember to get it into the freezer the day before, as it needs a good 24 hours for the crystals to form. The high vodka content prevents it from freezing into a solid block, so there's no need to stir it at all while it's in the freezer.

juice of 12 blood oranges

1¾ cups vodka

2 inches fresh ginger, peeled

6 tablespoons sugar

juice of 2 limes

Serves 4

1

Mix the blood orange juice and vodka in a large freezer-proof container. Grate the ginger into a bowl, then squeeze out the juice into the vodka mixture and discard the squeezed gratings. Stir the sugar and lime juice into the blood orange mixture until fully dissolved.

2

Freeze overnight. Next morning, mix with a spoon to break up the crystals. Return to the freezer. Serve in chilled ceramic or glass beakers or in tall stemmed glasses (chill them in the freezer).

Vanilla citrus salad with warm doughnuts

Pomelos are not dissimilar to grapefruit, just much bigger. The patterned skin encases a thick white pith which houses a compact fist of citrus segments made up of succulent filaments. You could try using ugli fruit instead (also known as hoogli fruit) or if you can't get either, use an extra grapefruit.

4 tablespoons superfine sugar

¼ cup honey

1 vanilla bean, split lengthwise

juice of 2 oranges

2 lemons, a strip of peel from 1 and the juice of both

2 limes, a strip of peel from 1 and the juice of both

2 pink or regular grapefruit

1 pomelo or grapefruit

1 tablespoon orange flower water

4 ring doughnuts, to serve

Serves 4

1

Put the sugar, honey, vanilla bean, orange juice, and lemon and lime zest and juice in a saucepan with 1¼ cups water. Simmer until reduced by about one-third.

2

Slice the peel from the grapefruit and pomelo, then slice out the segments, leaving the membranes behind. Immerse the citrus segments in the compote syrup, stir in the orange flower water and let cool.

3

Warm the doughnuts and compote. Put the doughnuts in 4 bowls and saturate with the compote syrup. Spoon over the citrus fruit and serve.

Variations:

• Serve the compote with pancakes, or with soft cheese beaten with a little sugar or over pancakes.

• To make a mock rum baba, flavor with dark rum instead of orange flower water.

Bananas, pineapples, and mangoes are now available all year round. They almost seem like natives. But there are others appearing more and more in our markets—lychees and papayas, kiwifruit and tamarillos, starfruit and rambutans. In fact these tropical fruits put me in mind of vacations and a whole host of traveling experiences: white sands, palms, heat, and vacation-brochure-blue waters. We now no longer have to wait to return to a far-flung destination to re-live the sensual delights of a breakfast of sweet papaya with lime or a shake made with red banana and vanilla. These exotics, and many more, are flown into our markets weekly—particularly welcome during winter when things are a little scarce on the home-grown front. We can create our own slice of tropicana with some of the more unusual fruits. Starfruit (carambola) has a sour sweetness even when ripe and is best used in dishes with sweet, spicy, and sour flavors. Lychees have translucent, perfumed white

flesh—much more delicious fresh than canned. Tamarillos (tree tomatoes) have intense ruby-rich flesh, sweet yet tart, so need added sugar (remove the very bitter skin). Then there's the humble-looking kiwifruit or Chinese gooseberry—underneath that mouse-brown skin is succulent green flesh.

Of all tropical fruits however, mangoes are the most versatile and my favorite. You just can't go wrong with them. Underipe or overripe they still have their uses—in chile salsas with broiled meat or fish, in salads, as caramelized tarts and sorbets, or eaten just as they are, running with juice straight from the skin—excellent.

cal fruits

Green fruit gado gado salad

with whole lime and peanut sauce

Classic Indonesian gado gado is a salad of blanched shredded vegetables, cucumber, and hard-cooked eggs with a sweet, hot, peanut sauce. Unripe (known as green) papaya and mango are common to Asian salads—they're best when finely shredded and tenderized with heavily lime-juiced dressings.

⅔ cup skinned unsalted peanuts, roughly crushed

1 garlic clove

½ teaspoon salt

2 small red chiles, seeded and chopped

6 tablespoons brown sugar or palm sugar

4 limes

½ tablespoon sugar

selection of sour fruits, such as green (unripe) mango, green (unripe) papaya, starfruit, or cucumber, peeled, pitted or seeded, and shredded* as necessary

a handful of basil, cilantro, and mint leaves

Serves 6 as an appetizer

Note: *A mandoline is the best tool for shredding the fruits or cucumbers.*

1

Dry-roast the crushed peanuts in a hot skillet until toasted and flecked with brown all over.

2

Using a mortar and pestle pound the garlic and salt until crushed to a purée. Add the chiles and pound until mashed. Pound in the sugar, then the toasted peanuts (if your mortar is full, do in batches). Don't grind all the peanuts to fine granules: some should remain coarsely crushed. Stir in the juice of 2 limes (use a little juice earlier if the mixture is too stiff to work).

3

Mix the sugar with the juice of 1 lime until dissolved. Toss the prepared fruits and herbs in the sweetened lime juice.

4

Cut the skin and pith from the remaining lime and slice out the segments from the surrounding membrane.

5

To assemble the salad, put small mounds of the sour fruit and herb salad on each dish (I use a 2-pronged carving fork to twist the salad like spaghetti). Top with the chile peanut sauce and cover loosely with more salad and lime segments.

Variations:

• Eat the salad and peanut dressing wrapped up in lettuce leaves.

• Add freshly grated or shavings of coconut.

• Serve on banana petals with chopsticks (page 3)—purple banana flowers are available from specialty Asian food shops.

Mango lapsang chicken

and herb salad with honey and sesame dressing

To slice a mango in half you must cut parallel to the elliptical flat side of the seed. It's not as complicated as it sounds. The outward shape mirrors the internal seed—always cut lengthwise with the mango positioned narrow end down. When you hit the seed, slice around it as you cut through. For this recipe choose firm fruit—too ripe and the flesh will disintegrate as you slice.

½ cooked chicken, cut in half

2 tablespoons rice vinegar

1 tablespoon sugar

1 garlic clove

1 bird's eye chile, very finely chopped

shredded curly endive, fresh rinsed bean sprouts, or baby spinach

4 scallions, trimmed and shredded

2 handfuls cilantro, mint, and basil leaves

1 very large firm mango, peeled, sides sliced off parallel to the seed, then cut into wafer-thin slices

2 tablespoons black (or white) sesame seeds, toasted in a dry skillet

Smoking mixture (optional):

¼ cup Lapsang souchong tea leaves

3 tablespoons brown sugar

3 tablespoons uncooked rice

Honey and sesame dressing:

5 tablespoons honey

3 tablespoons rice vinegar

½ cup peanut oil

2 teaspoons sesame oil

Serves 4 as a light lunch, 8 as an appetizer

1

To smoke the chicken, line the base of a steamer with a double thickness of foil. Spread the smoking mixture ingredients over the foil. Put the chicken in the steaming tray, assemble the steamer and cover with a lid. Place over a gentle heat until the smoke rises and smoke for about 20 minutes. Alternatively, omit the smoking step and use plain cooked chicken.

2

Mix the rice vinegar, sugar, garlic, and chile and stir until the sugar has dissolved.

3

Discard the chicken skin (and smoking ingredients), flake the meat from the bone, and toss with the rice vinegar mixture.

4

To make the dressing, put the honey and vinegar in a food processor and blend. Gradually add the peanut and sesame oils through the feed tube of the processor, until fully emulsified, as if making mayonnaise. The dressing should be of sauce consistency. Use half for this salad and use the remainder for other dishes.

5

Mix the chicken with the endive, bean sprouts, or spinach, then add the scallions, cilantro, mint, and basil. Put neat piles onto plates or into bowls, then serve topped with sliced mango, the honey and sesame dressing, and the toasted sesame seeds.

Tamarillo cassata with lychee and papaya

This is fabulous. And will win over people unsure of the tang of the tamarillo (also known as tree tomato). The different ices must be made up separately, semi-frozen, then layered (or you could just make the tamarillo ice and serve it with crème fraîche and shavings of fresh coconut). The cassata is easy to make, but will demand your presence for a day—there's some to-ing and fro-ing from the freezer, so start well in advance. Halve the quantities if you prefer, though it's good to have extra available when you feel a "cassata moment" take hold (which you will after trying this one). It will keep in the freezer for about 2 months.

Papaya ice:

7 chilled limes, zest of 1 and juice of all

1¼ cups confectioners' sugar

3 ripe papayas, peeled and seeded, giving about 1½ lb. flesh

Lychee ice cream:

50 lychees, peeled and seeded

⅔ cup confectioners' sugar

1½ cups crème fraîche

6 glacé cherries

Tamarillo ice:

2 chilled blood oranges or regular oranges, finely grated zest of 1, juice of both

12 ripe tamarillos, quartered, flesh filleted from skin (discard the skin)

1¾ cups confectioners' sugar

Makes 10–12 large slices

1

To make the papaya ice, blend the lime juice, lime zest, and confectioners' sugar and set aside for about 30 minutes. Transfer to a food processor, add the papaya flesh, and blend to a purée. Transfer to a plastic container and put in the freezer until semi-frozen. Return the mixture to the processor, blend to a purée, then freeze again. Before it sets, blend it once more, and spoon this time into a container about 6 x 8 inches, smooth level, then freeze hard.

2

To make the lychee ice cream, put the lychee flesh in a food processor, add the sugar, and blend to a purée. Add the crème fraîche and blend again. Transfer to a plastic container and put in the freezer until semi-frozen. Blend and freeze once more, as for papaya ice. Before it sets finally, blend it once more, then spoon over the top of the frozen papaya ice. Push cherries randomly into the lychee ice cream and let freeze until set.

3

To make the tamarillo ice, blend the orange juice with the orange zest and confectioners' sugar and set aside for 30 minutes. Transfer to a food processor, add the tamarillo flesh, and blend to a purée. Taste—if too sharp, add a little extra sugar. Transfer to a plastic container and put in the freezer until semi-frozen. Proceed as above and add as the final layer to the cassata. Freeze overnight. Before serving, let stand at room temperature for about 5 minutes, turn out onto a freezer-chilled platter or board, then slice. To slow down the melting process, serve on freezer-chilled plates.

Jacket bananas

with cardamom orange syrup and crème fraîche

Bananas are utterly wonderful baked. And need no preparation—they come ready-wrapped in their own skins and can be baked as they are on the oven shelf. Such a convenient bunch. And this, so friends tell me, is the best banana dessert in the world.

4 bananas, unpeeled

20 green cardamom pods, black seeds removed and lightly bruised (discard husks)

juice of 4 oranges

juice of 2 lemons

½ cup light brown sugar

½ cup sugar or vanilla sugar

⅓ cup brandy (optional)

crème fraîche, to serve

Serves 4

1

Bake the bananas in a preheated oven at 400°F for about 25 minutes or until skin is black and the banana yields when prodded.

2

Meanwhile, put all the remaining ingredients except the crème fraîche in a saucepan and simmer until reduced to a thin syrup.

3

Split the bananas open, pour over the cardamom orange syrup, and top with crème fraîche.

Passion cake

You wouldn't look twice at a passionfruit—that's if you didn't know what lay within. It looks far from passionate. The flower is extremely distinctive and this gives rise to its name, symbolizing the Passion of Christ. But the plainest of fruits contains within its hallowed skin a richly perfumed nectar-like mass of juices and seeds (which are edible too). Truly humble on the outside and full of heaven-sent things within—halve, scoop out the contents, and enjoy.

1¼ cups ground almonds

6½ tablespoons all-purpose flour, sifted

a pinch of salt

4 eggs, separated

1 vanilla bean, split lengthwise

¾ cup superfine sugar

strained flesh and juice of 6 passionfruit

2 tablespoons confectioner's sugar

Passionfruit syrup:

flesh and seeds of 8 passionfruit

juice of ½ lemon

½ cup sugar

thick double cream or crème fraîche, to serve

Makes 8 individual heart-shaped cakes

eight 4-inch heart-shaped cake pans, greased and base-lined

1

Mix the ground almonds in a bowl with the flour and salt, and make a well in the center. In a second bowl, beat the egg yolks with the sugar until the mixture is pale and leaves a trail when lifted. Scrape the seeds from the vanilla bean into the mixture, and beat well. Stir into the almond mixture, followed by the passionfruit juice.

2

Beat the egg whites to soft peak stage and fold into the cake mixture. Divide between 8 greased and base-lined 4-inch heart-shaped tins and bake in a preheated oven at 350°F for 15—20 minutes until the cake spring back when lightly pressed. Turn out and let cool on a wire rack.

3

Put all the syrup ingredients in a small saucepan and heat to make a thin syrup. Lightly dust the cakes with confectioners' sugar and serve in a pool of syrup with double cream or créme fraîche.

Variation:

• Make a large cake, cool and slice into 3 layers. Fill each layer with mascarpone flavored with lemon curd.

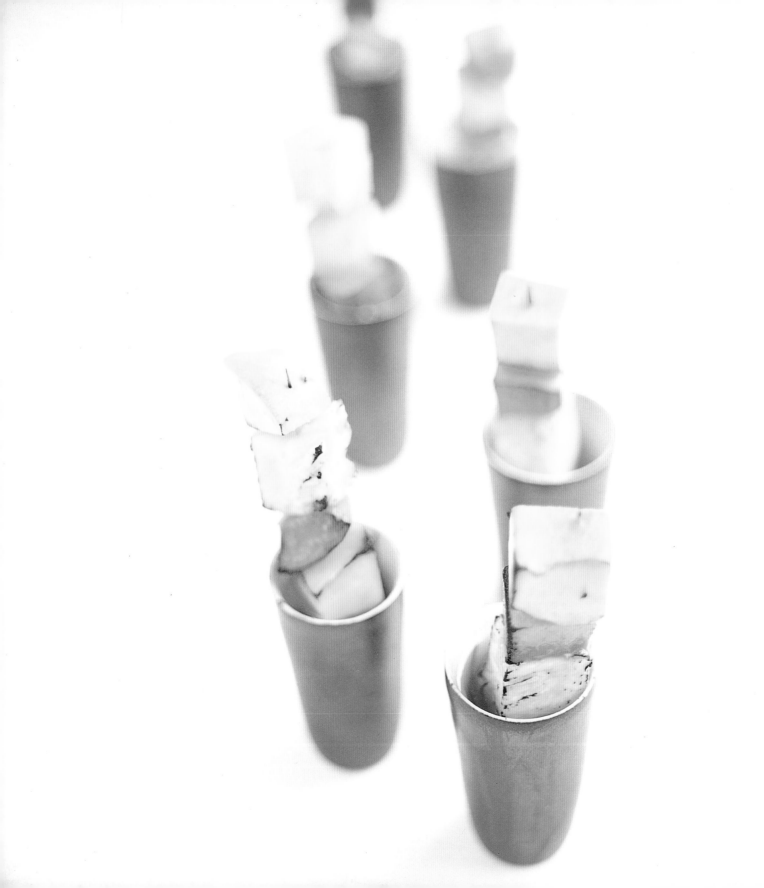

Rum fruit skewers with lime syrup

A grilled fruit salad with that totally tropical taste, caramelized with rum and molasses-rich sugar. Pineapple is made for this dish—in fact you could use just pineapple if you like, and grill in wedges rather than on skewers.

1 small pineapple

1 mango

1 papaya

¼ cup dark brown sugar or palm sugar, if available

¼ cup dark rum

4 limes

1 cup superfine sugar

Serves 4–6

1

Peel all the fruits, deseed or core, then cut into equally sized chunks. Thread onto bamboo or small metal skewers and fit into a shallow dish. The fruit can be trimmed into cubes after threading onto skewers, as pictured.

2

Sprinkle with sugar and rum and set aside for about 1 hour.

3

To make the lime syrup, peel the zest from the limes (without taking any of the white pith) and slice into fine strips. Squeeze the juice from the peeled limes and put with the strips of zest, sugar, and ¼ cup water in a small saucepan. Bring to a boil, then reduce the heat and simmer until reduced to a thin syrup. Let cool.

4

Blister the fruit skewers under a very hot broiler or sear in a preheated heavy-bottom skillet (or use a cook's blow torch). Serve coated with the lime syrup or plunged into narrow cups filled with the syrup.

Variations:

• Use kaffir limes if you can get them. Add a dash of chopped chile to the lime syrup.

• Serve the broiled fruit with vanilla, lime, or coconut ice cream.

index